SCOTLAND

Address Book

LOMOND

Loch Shiel and Glenfinnan Monument, Lochaber, Highlands.

Name

Address

Tel/Fax

Mobile

Email

Name

Address

Tel/Fax

Mobile

Email

Name

Address

Tel/Fax

Mobile

Email

Name

Address

Tel/Fax

Mobile

Email

Name

Address

Tel/Fax

Mobile

Email

Name

Address

Tel/Fax

Mobile

Email

Name

Address

Tel/Fax

Mobile

Email

Name

Address

Tel/Fax

Mobile

Email

Name

Address

Tel/Fax

Mobile

Email

a

a

Name	Name	Name
Address	Address	Address
Tel/Fax	Tel/Fax	Tel/Fax
Mobile	Mobile	Mobile
Email	Email	Email

Name	Name	Name
Address	Address	Address
Tel/Fax	Tel/Fax	Tel/Fax
Mobile	Mobile	Mobile
Email	Email	Email

Name	Name	Name
Address	Address	Address
Tel/Fax	Tel/Fax	Tel/Fax
Mobile	Mobile	Mobile
Email	Email	Email

Name	Name	Name
Address	Address	Address
Tel/Fax	Tel/Fax	Tel/Fax
Mobile	Mobile	Mobile
Email	Email	Email
Name	Name	Name
Address	Address	Address
Tel/Fax	Tel/Fax	Tel/Fax
Mobile	Mobile	Mobile
Email	Email	Email
Name	Name	Name
Address	Address	Address
Tel/Fax	Tel/Fax	Tel/Fax
Mobile	Mobile	Mobile
Email	Email	Email

a

Kiloran Bay, Colonsay.

Name

Address

Tel/Fax

Mobile

Email

Name

Address

Tel/Fax

Mobile

Email

Name

Address

Tel/Fax

Mobile

Email

Name

Address

Tel/Fax

Mobile

Email

Name

Address

Tel/Fax

Mobile

Email

Name

Address

Tel/Fax

Mobile

Email

Name

Address

Tel/Fax

Mobile

Email

Name

Address

Tel/Fax

Mobile

Email

Name

Address

Tel/Fax

Mobile

Email

b

b

Name

Address

Tel/Fax

Mobile

Email

Name

Address

Tel/Fax

Mobile

Email

Name

Address

Tel/Fax

Mobile

Email

Name

Address

Tel/Fax

Mobile

Email

Name

Address

Tel/Fax

Mobile

Email

Name

Address

Tel/Fax

Mobile

Email

Name

Address

Tel/Fax

Mobile

Email

Name

Address

Tel/Fax

Mobile

Email

Name

Address

Tel/Fax

Mobile

Email

Name

Address

Tel/Fax

Mobile

Email

Name

Address

Tel/Fax

Mobile

Email

Name

Address

Tel/Fax

Mobile

Email

Name

Address

Tel/Fax

Mobile

Email

Name

Address

Tel/Fax

Mobile

Email

Name

Address

Tel/Fax

Mobile

Email

Name

Address

Tel/Fax

Mobile

Email

Name

Address

Tel/Fax

Mobile

Email

Name

Address

Tel/Fax

Mobile

Email

b

Looking towards Cape Wrath from Faraid Head, Sutherland.

Name

Address

Tel/Fax

Mobile

Email

Name

Address

Tel/Fax

Mobile

Email

Name

Address

Tel/Fax

Mobile

Email

Name

Address

Tel/Fax

Mobile

Email

Name

Address

Tel/Fax

Mobile

Email

Name

Address

Tel/Fax

Mobile

Email

Name

Address

Tel/Fax

Mobile

Email

Name

Address

Tel/Fax

Mobile

Email

Name

Address

Tel/Fax

Mobile

Email

C

C

Name

Address

Tel/Fax

Mobile

Email

Name

Address

Tel/Fax

Mobile

Email

Name

Address

Tel/Fax

Mobile

Email

Name

Address

Tel/Fax

Mobile

Email

Name

Address

Tel/Fax

Mobile

Email

Name

Address

Tel/Fax

Mobile

Email

Name

Address

Tel/Fax

Mobile

Email

Name

Address

Tel/Fax

Mobile

Email

Name

Address

Tel/Fax

Mobile

Email

Name

Address

Tel/Fax

Mobile

Email

Name

Address

Tel/Fax

Mobile

Email

Name

Address

Tel/Fax

Mobile

Email

Name

Address

Tel/Fax

Mobile

Email

Name

Address

Tel/Fax

Mobile

Email

Name

Address

Tel/Fax

Mobile

Email

Name

Address

Tel/Fax

Mobile

Email

Name

Address

Tel/Fax

Mobile

Email

Name

Address

Tel/Fax

Mobile

Email

C

Edinburgh Castle and City.

Name

Address

Tel/Fax

Mobile

Email

Name

Address

Tel/Fax

Mobile

Email

Name

Address

Tel/Fax

Mobile

Email

Name

Address

Tel/Fax

Mobile

Email

Name

Address

Tel/Fax

Mobile

Email

Name

Address

Tel/Fax

Mobile

Email

Name

Address

Tel/Fax

Mobile

Email

Name

Address

Tel/Fax

Mobile

Email

Name

Address

Tel/Fax

Mobile

Email

d

d

Name	Name	Name
Address	Address	Address
Tel/Fax	Tel/Fax	Tel/Fax
Mobile	Mobile	Mobile
Email	Email	Email
Name	Name	Name
Address	Address	Address
Tel/Fax	Tel/Fax	Tel/Fax
Mobile	Mobile	Mobile
Email	Email	Email
Name	Name	Name
Address	Address	Address
Tel/Fax	Tel/Fax	Tel/Fax
Mobile	Mobile	Mobile
Email	Email	Email

Name	Name	Name
Address	Address	Address
Tel/Fax	Tel/Fax	Tel/Fax
Mobile	Mobile	Mobile
Email	Email	Email
Name	Name	Name
Address	Address	Address
Tel/Fax	Tel/Fax	Tel/Fax
Mobile	Mobile	Mobile
Email	Email	Email
Name	Name	Name
Address	Address	Address
Tel/Fax	Tel/Fax	Tel/Fax
Mobile	Mobile	Mobile
Email	Email	Email

d

Loch Lomond – with the Islands of Inchcailloch and Clairinsh in the foreground.

Name

Address

Tel/Fax

Mobile

Email

Name

Address

Tel/Fax

Mobile

Email

Name

Address

Tel/Fax

Mobile

Email

Name

Address

Tel/Fax

Mobile

Email

Name

Address

Tel/Fax

Mobile

Email

Name

Address

Tel/Fax

Mobile

Email

Name

Address

Tel/Fax

Mobile

Email

e

Name

Address

Tel/Fax

Mobile

Email

Name

Address

Tel/Fax

Mobile

Email

e

Name	Name	Name
Address	Address	Address
Tel/Fax	Tel/Fax	Tel/Fax
Mobile	Mobile	Mobile
Email	Email	Email
Name	Name	Name
Address	Address	Address
Tel/Fax	Tel/Fax	Tel/Fax
Mobile	Mobile	Mobile
Email	Email	Email
Name	Name	Name
Address	Address	Address
Tel/Fax	Tel/Fax	Tel/Fax
Mobile	Mobile	Mobile
Email	Email	Email

Name

Address

Tel/Fax

Mobile

Email

Name

Address

Tel/Fax

Mobile

Email

Name

Address

Tel/Fax

Mobile

Email

Name

Address

Tel/Fax

Mobile

Email

Name

Address

Tel/Fax

Mobile

Email

Name

Address

Tel/Fax

Mobile

Email

Name

Address

Tel/Fax

Mobile

Email

Name

Address

Tel/Fax

Mobile

Email

Name

Address

Tel/Fax

Mobile

Email

f

Traigh Bàn nam Manach, Iona

Name	Name	Name
Address	Address	Address
Tel/Fax	Tel/Fax	Tel/Fax
Mobile	Mobile	Mobile
Email	Email	Email
Name	Name	Name
Address	Address	Address
Tel/Fax	Tel/Fax	Tel/Fax
Mobile	Mobile	Mobile
Email	Email	Email
Name	Name	Name
Address	Address	Address
Tel/Fax	Tel/Fax	Tel/Fax
Mobile	Mobile	Mobile
Email	Email	Email

g

g

Name	Name	Name
Address	Address	Address
Tel/Fax	Tel/Fax	Tel/Fax
Mobile	Mobile	Mobile
Email	Email	Email
Name	Name	Name
Address	Address	Address
Tel/Fax	Tel/Fax	Tel/Fax
Mobile	Mobile	Mobile
Email	Email	Email
Name	Name	Name
Address	Address	Address
Tel/Fax	Tel/Fax	Tel/Fax
Mobile	Mobile	Mobile
Email	Email	Email

Name	Name	Name
Address	Address	Address
Tel/Fax	Tel/Fax	Tel/Fax
Mobile	Mobile	Mobile
Email	Email	Email
Name	Name	Name
Address	Address	Address
Tel/Fax	Tel/Fax	Tel/Fax
Mobile	Mobile	Mobile
Email	Email	Email
Name	Name	Name
Address	Address	Address
Tel/Fax	Tel/Fax	Tel/Fax
Mobile	Mobile	Mobile
Email	Email	Email

g

Loch Tummel and Schiehallion, Perthshire.

Name

Address

Tel/Fax

Mobile

Email

Name

Address

Tel/Fax

Mobile

Email

Name

Address

Tel/Fax

Mobile

Email

Name

Address

Tel/Fax

Mobile

Email

Name

Address

Tel/Fax

Mobile

Email

Name

Address

Tel/Fax

Mobile

Email

Name

Address

Tel/Fax

Mobile

Email

Name

Address

Tel/Fax

Mobile

Email

Name

Address

Tel/Fax

Mobile

Email

h

h

Name	Name	Name
Address	Address	Address
Tel/Fax	Tel/Fax	Tel/Fax
Mobile	Mobile	Mobile
Email	Email	Email

Name	Name	Name
Address	Address	Address
Tel/Fax	Tel/Fax	Tel/Fax
Mobile	Mobile	Mobile
Email	Email	Email

Name	Name	Name
Address	Address	Address
Tel/Fax	Tel/Fax	Tel/Fax
Mobile	Mobile	Mobile
Email	Email	Email

Name	Name	Name
Address	Address	Address
Tel/Fax	Tel/Fax	Tel/Fax
Mobile	Mobile	Mobile
Email	Email	Email

Name	Name	Name
Address	Address	Address
Tel/Fax	Tel/Fax	Tel/Fax
Mobile	Mobile	Mobile
Email	Email	Email

Name	Name	Name
Address	Address	Address
Tel/Fax	Tel/Fax	Tel/Fax
Mobile	Mobile	Mobile
Email	Email	Email

i

Looking across Inner Sound towards Raasay & Skye from Ardban, Wester Ross.

Name

Address

Tel/Fax

Mobile

Email

Name

Address

Tel/Fax

Mobile

Email

Name

Address

Tel/Fax

Mobile

Email

Name

Address

Tel/Fax

Mobile

Email

Name

Address

Tel/Fax

Mobile

Email

Name

Address

Tel/Fax

Mobile

Email

Name

Address

Tel/Fax

Mobile

Email

Name

Address

Tel/Fax

Mobile

Email

Name

Address

Tel/Fax

Mobile

Email

j

j

Name	Name	Name
Address	Address	Address
Tel/Fax	Tel/Fax	Tel/Fax
Mobile	Mobile	Mobile
Email	Email	Email
Name	Name	Name
Address	Address	Address
Tel/Fax	Tel/Fax	Tel/Fax
Mobile	Mobile	Mobile
Email	Email	Email
Name	Name	Name
Address	Address	Address
Tel/Fax	Tel/Fax	Tel/Fax
Mobile	Mobile	Mobile
Email	Email	Email

Name	Name	Name
Address	Address	Address
Tel/Fax	Tel/Fax	Tel/Fax
Mobile	Mobile	Mobile
Email	Email	Email
Name	Name	Name
Address	Address	Address
Tel/Fax	Tel/Fax	Tel/Fax
Mobile	Mobile	Mobile
Email	Email	Email
Name	Name	Name
Address	Address	Address
Tel/Fax	Tel/Fax	Tel/Fax
Mobile	Mobile	Mobile
Email	Email	Email

k

Strathspey from the foothills of the Cairngorms, Highlands.

Name

Address

Tel/Fax

Mobile

Email

Name

Address

Tel/Fax

Mobile

Email

Name

Address

Tel/Fax

Mobile

Email

Name

Address

Tel/Fax

Mobile

Email

Name

Address

Tel/Fax

Mobile

Email

Name

Address

Tel/Fax

Mobile

Email

Name

Address

Tel/Fax

Mobile

Email

Name

Address

Tel/Fax

Mobile

Email

Name

Address

Tel/Fax

Mobile

Email

l

l

Name

Address

Tel/Fax

Mobile

Email

Name

Address

Tel/Fax

Mobile

Email

Name

Address

Tel/Fax

Mobile

Email

Name

Address

Tel/Fax

Mobile

Email

Name

Address

Tel/Fax

Mobile

Email

Name

Address

Tel/Fax

Mobile

Email

Name

Address

Tel/Fax

Mobile

Email

Name

Address

Tel/Fax

Mobile

Email

Name

Address

Tel/Fax

Mobile

Email

Name	Name	Name
Address	Address	Address
Tel/Fax	Tel/Fax	Tel/Fax
Mobile	Mobile	Mobile
Email	Email	Email
Name	Name	Name
Address	Address	Address
Tel/Fax	Tel/Fax	Tel/Fax
Mobile	Mobile	Mobile
Email	Email	Email
Name	Name	Name
Address	Address	Address
Tel/Fax	Tel/Fax	Tel/Fax
Mobile	Mobile	Mobile
Email	Email	Email

Loch Assynt, Sutherland.

Name

Address

Tel/Fax

Mobile

Email

Name

Address

Tel/Fax

Mobile

Email

Name

Address

Tel/Fax

Mobile

Email

Name

Address

Tel/Fax

Mobile

Email

Name

Address

Tel/Fax

Mobile

Email

Name

Address

Tel/Fax

Mobile

Email

Name

Address

Tel/Fax

Mobile

Email

Name

Address

Tel/Fax

Mobile

Email

Name

Address

Tel/Fax

Mobile

Email

m

m

Name	Name	Name
Address	Address	Address
Tel/Fax	Tel/Fax	Tel/Fax
Mobile	Mobile	Mobile
Email	Email	Email

Name	Name	Name
Address	Address	Address
Tel/Fax	Tel/Fax	Tel/Fax
Mobile	Mobile	Mobile
Email	Email	Email

Name	Name	Name
Address	Address	Address
Tel/Fax	Tel/Fax	Tel/Fax
Mobile	Mobile	Mobile
Email	Email	Email

Name	Name	Name
Address	Address	Address
Tel/Fax	Tel/Fax	Tel/Fax
Mobile	Mobile	Mobile
Email	Email	Email
Name	Name	Name
Address	Address	Address
Tel/Fax	Tel/Fax	Tel/Fax
Mobile	Mobile	Mobile
Email	Email	Email
Name	Name	Name
Address	Address	Address
Tel/Fax	Tel/Fax	Tel/Fax
Mobile	Mobile	Mobile
Email	Email	Email

m

Kilchurn Castle, Loch Awe, Argyll.

Name

Address

Tel/Fax

Mobile

Email

Name

Address

Tel/Fax

Mobile

Email

Name

Address

Tel/Fax

Mobile

Email

Name

Address

Tel/Fax

Mobile

Email

Name

Address

Tel/Fax

Mobile

Email

Name

Address

Tel/Fax

Mobile

Email

Name

Address

Tel/Fax

Mobile

Email

Name

Address

Tel/Fax

Mobile

Email

Name

Address

Tel/Fax

Mobile

Email

mac mc

mac
mc

Name

Address

Tel/Fax

Mobile

Email

Name

Address

Tel/Fax

Mobile

Email

Name

Address

Tel/Fax

Mobile

Email

Name

Address

Tel/Fax

Mobile

Email

Name

Address

Tel/Fax

Mobile

Email

Name

Address

Tel/Fax

Mobile

Email

Name

Address

Tel/Fax

Mobile

Email

Name

Address

Tel/Fax

Mobile

Email

Name

Address

Tel/Fax

Mobile

Email

Name	Name	Name
Address	Address	Address
Tel/Fax	Tel/Fax	Tel/Fax
Mobile	Mobile	Mobile
Email	Email	Email

mac
mc

Name	Name	Name
Address	Address	Address
Tel/Fax	Tel/Fax	Tel/Fax
Mobile	Mobile	Mobile
Email	Email	Email

Name	Name	Name
Address	Address	Address
Tel/Fax	Tel/Fax	Tel/Fax
Mobile	Mobile	Mobile
Email	Email	Email

The West Coast of Harris, Western Isles.

Name

Address

Tel/Fax

Mobile

Email

Name

Address

Tel/Fax

Mobile

Email

Name

Address

Tel/Fax

Mobile

Email

Name

Address

Tel/Fax

Mobile

Email

Name

Address

Tel/Fax

Mobile

Email

Name

Address

Tel/Fax

Mobile

Email

Name

Address

Tel/Fax

Mobile

Email

Name

Address

Tel/Fax

Mobile

Email

Name

Address

Tel/Fax

Mobile

Email

n

n

Name	Name	Name
Address	Address	Address
Tel/Fax	Tel/Fax	Tel/Fax
Mobile	Mobile	Mobile
Email	Email	Email

Name	Name	Name
Address	Address	Address
Tel/Fax	Tel/Fax	Tel/Fax
Mobile	Mobile	Mobile
Email	Email	Email

Name	Name	Name
Address	Address	Address
Tel/Fax	Tel/Fax	Tel/Fax
Mobile	Mobile	Mobile
Email	Email	Email

Name	Name	Name
Address	Address	Address
Tel/Fax	Tel/Fax	Tel/Fax
Mobile	Mobile	Mobile
Email	Email	Email
Name	Name	Name
Address	Address	Address
Tel/Fax	Tel/Fax	Tel/Fax
Mobile	Mobile	Mobile
Email	Email	Email
Name	Name	Name
Address	Address	Address
Tel/Fax	Tel/Fax	Tel/Fax
Mobile	Mobile	Mobile
Email	Email	Email

Gaada Stack, Foula, Shetland.

Name

Address

Tel/Fax

Mobile

Email

Name

Address

Tel/Fax

Mobile

Email

Name

Address

Tel/Fax

Mobile

Email

Name

Address

Tel/Fax

Mobile

Email

Name

Address

Tel/Fax

Mobile

Email

Name

Address

Tel/Fax

Mobile

Email

Name

Address

Tel/Fax

Mobile

Email

Name

Address

Tel/Fax

Mobile

Email

Name

Address

Tel/Fax

Mobile

Email

p

p

Name
Address

Tel/Fax
Mobile
Email

Name
Address

Tel/Fax
Mobile
Email

Name
Address

Tel/Fax
Mobile
Email

Name
Address

Tel/Fax
Mobile
Email

Name
Address

Tel/Fax
Mobile
Email

Name
Address

Tel/Fax
Mobile
Email

Name
Address

Tel/Fax
Mobile
Email

Name
Address

Tel/Fax
Mobile
Email

Name
Address

Tel/Fax
Mobile
Email

Name

Address

Tel/Fax

Mobile

Email

Name

Address

Tel/Fax

Mobile

Email

Name

Address

Tel/Fax

Mobile

Email

Name

Address

Tel/Fax

Mobile

Email

Name

Address

Tel/Fax

Mobile

Email

Name

Address

Tel/Fax

Mobile

Email

Name

Address

Tel/Fax

Mobile

Email

Name

Address

Tel/Fax

Mobile

Email

Name

Address

Tel/Fax

Mobile

Email

q

Buachaille Etive Mór, Glencoe.

Name

Address

Tel/Fax

Mobile

Email

Name

Address

Tel/Fax

Mobile

Email

Name

Address

Tel/Fax

Mobile

Email

Name

Address

Tel/Fax

Mobile

Email

Name

Address

Tel/Fax

Mobile

Email

Name

Address

Tel/Fax

Mobile

Email

Name

Address

Tel/Fax

Mobile

Email

Name

Address

Tel/Fax

Mobile

Email

Name

Address

Tel/Fax

Mobile

Email

r

r

Name

Address

Tel/Fax

Mobile

Email

Name

Address

Tel/Fax

Mobile

Email

Name

Address

Tel/Fax

Mobile

Email

Name

Address

Tel/Fax

Mobile

Email

Name

Address

Tel/Fax

Mobile

Email

Name

Address

Tel/Fax

Mobile

Email

Name

Address

Tel/Fax

Mobile

Email

Name

Address

Tel/Fax

Mobile

Email

Name

Address

Tel/Fax

Mobile

Email

Name

Address

Tel/Fax

Mobile

Email

Name

Address

Tel/Fax

Mobile

Email

Name

Address

Tel/Fax

Mobile

Email

Name

Address

Tel/Fax

Mobile

Email

Name

Address

Tel/Fax

Mobile

Email

Name

Address

Tel/Fax

Mobile

Email

Name

Address

Tel/Fax

Mobile

Email

Name

Address

Tel/Fax

Mobile

Email

Name

Address

Tel/Fax

Mobile

Email

r

River Avon, Strath Avon, Moray.

Name	Name	Name
Address	Address	Address
Tel/Fax	Tel/Fax	Tel/Fax
Mobile	Mobile	Mobile
Email	Email	Email
Name	Name	Name
Address	Address	Address
Tel/Fax	Tel/Fax	Tel/Fax
Mobile	Mobile	Mobile
Email	Email	Email
Name	Name	Name
Address	Address	Address
Tel/Fax	Tel/Fax	Tel/Fax
Mobile	Mobile	Mobile
Email	Email	Email

S

S

Name	Name	Name
Address	Address	Address
Tel/Fax	Tel/Fax	Tel/Fax
Mobile	Mobile	Mobile
Email	Email	Email

Name	Name	Name
Address	Address	Address
Tel/Fax	Tel/Fax	Tel/Fax
Mobile	Mobile	Mobile
Email	Email	Email

Name	Name	Name
Address	Address	Address
Tel/Fax	Tel/Fax	Tel/Fax
Mobile	Mobile	Mobile
Email	Email	Email

Name

Address

Tel/Fax

Mobile

Email

Name

Address

Tel/Fax

Mobile

Email

Name

Address

Tel/Fax

Mobile

Email

Name

Address

Tel/Fax

Mobile

Email

Name

Address

Tel/Fax

Mobile

Email

Name

Address

Tel/Fax

Mobile

Email

Name

Address

Tel/Fax

Mobile

Email

Name

Address

Tel/Fax

Mobile

Email

Name

Address

Tel/Fax

Mobile

Email

S

Blair Castle, Perthshire.

Name

Address

Tel/Fax

Mobile

Email

Name

Address

Tel/Fax

Mobile

Email

Name

Address

Tel/Fax

Mobile

Email

Name

Address

Tel/Fax

Mobile

Email

Name

Address

Tel/Fax

Mobile

Email

Name

Address

Tel/Fax

Mobile

Email

Name

Address

Tel/Fax

Mobile

Email

Name

Address

Tel/Fax

Mobile

Email

Name

Address

Tel/Fax

Mobile

Email

t

t

Name	Name	Name
Address	Address	Address
Tel/Fax	Tel/Fax	Tel/Fax
Mobile	Mobile	Mobile
Email	Email	Email
Name	Name	Name
Address	Address	Address
Tel/Fax	Tel/Fax	Tel/Fax
Mobile	Mobile	Mobile
Email	Email	Email
Name	Name	Name
Address	Address	Address
Tel/Fax	Tel/Fax	Tel/Fax
Mobile	Mobile	Mobile
Email	Email	Email

Name

Address

Tel/Fax

Mobile

Email

Name

Address

Tel/Fax

Mobile

Email

Name

Address

Tel/Fax

Mobile

Email

Name

Address

Tel/Fax

Mobile

Email

Name

Address

Tel/Fax

Mobile

Email

Name

Address

Tel/Fax

Mobile

Email

u
v

Name

Address

Tel/Fax

Mobile

Email

Name

Address

Tel/Fax

Mobile

Email

Name

Address

Tel/Fax

Mobile

Email

The Cuillin Hills and Loch Scavaig, Isle of Skye.

Name

Address

Tel/Fax

Mobile

Email

Name

Address

Tel/Fax

Mobile

Email

Name

Address

Tel/Fax

Mobile

Email

Name

Address

Tel/Fax

Mobile

Email

Name

Address

Tel/Fax

Mobile

Email

Name

Address

Tel/Fax

Mobile

Email

Name

Address

Tel/Fax

Mobile

Email

Name

Address

Tel/Fax

Mobile

Email

Name

Address

Tel/Fax

Mobile

Email

w

w

Name

Address

Tel/Fax

Mobile

Email

Name

Address

Tel/Fax

Mobile

Email

Name

Address

Tel/Fax

Mobile

Email

Name

Address

Tel/Fax

Mobile

Email

Name

Address

Tel/Fax

Mobile

Email

Name

Address

Tel/Fax

Mobile

Email

Name

Address

Tel/Fax

Mobile

Email

Name

Address

Tel/Fax

Mobile

Email

Name

Address

Tel/Fax

Mobile

Email

Name

Address

Tel/Fax

Mobile

Email

Name

Address

Tel/Fax

Mobile

Email

Name

Address

Tel/Fax

Mobile

Email

Name

Address

Tel/Fax

Mobile

Email

Name

Address

Tel/Fax

Mobile

Email

Name

Address

Tel/Fax

Mobile

Email

Name

Address

Tel/Fax

Mobile

Email

Name

Address

Tel/Fax

Mobile

Email

Name

Address

Tel/Fax

Mobile

Email

w

Pittenweem, Fife.

Name

Address

Tel/Fax

Mobile

Email

Name

Address

Tel/Fax

Mobile

Email

Name

Address

Tel/Fax

Mobile

Email

Name

Address

Tel/Fax

Mobile

Email

Name

Address

Tel/Fax

Mobile

Email

Name

Address

Tel/Fax

Mobile

Email

Name

Address

Tel/Fax

Mobile

Email

Name

Address

Tel/Fax

Mobile

Email

Name

Address

Tel/Fax

Mobile

Email

$y\,{}^{x}_{z}$

NOTES

Published by Lomond Books Ltd.

14 Freskyn Place, East Mains Industrial Estate, Broxburn, EH52 5NF

Produced by Colin Baxter Photography Ltd.

Photographs © Colin Baxter 2008

Front Cover Photograph: Loch Garten, Strathspey, Cairngorms National Park.
Back Cover Photograph: The Five Sisters of Kintail & Loch Duich, West Highlands.